BIRDS, BEES

AND STORKS

THE MAESTRO

THE HOFFNUNG SYMPHONY ORCHESTRA

THE HOFFNUNG MUSIC FESTIVAL

THE HOFFNUNG COMPANION TO MUSIC

HOFFNUNG'S MUSICAL CHAIRS

HOFFNUNG'S ACOUSTICS

HO HO HOFFNUNG

Birds, Bees

and

Storks

by

GERARD   HOFFNUNG

London

DENNIS DOBSON

Printed in Great Britain by
Metcalfe & Co. Ltd.,
Cambridge

I think . . . .

I do think . . . .

The time has come . . . .

Come along my boy . . . .

I want to have a talk with you.

It is a fact . . . .

Let's face it . . . .

After all, I am your father . . . .

Am I not ?

Life, my boy, is very mysterious . . . .

But we must look at it in a sensible way . . . .

What was I going to say ?

Oh yes . . . .

You know how flowers . . . .

In spring . . . .

And the birds . . . .

In their own way . . . .

Just let me think . . . .

And the bees too, of course . . . .

You see . . . .

I will try to explain . . . .

When *I* was young . . . .

I had to find out by myself . . . .

About girls . . . .

Nobody told *me* these things.

Now . . . .

The point is . . . .

Your mother . . . .

And I . . . .

I remember . . .

When we . . . .

Yes, well . . . .

That day . . . .

Was very hot . . . .

Like this one . . . .

But, I was saying, the birds and the bees and the butterflies . . . .

It's all perfectly clear . . . .

Isn't it?

Perhaps after all it's not such a mystery . . . .

You'd better not keep Felicity waiting . . . .

Goodbye my boy, I am very happy . . . .

To have had this little talk.

The factual approach . . . .

Is always the best.